Switch from PC to Mac

Step-by-step guide to set up and
get to know your new Mac

Marina Gallego López
http://www.marinagallego.com

SWITCH FROM PC TO MAC

Do you want to reduce the learning curve of moving to Mac to a couple of hours?
Do you want to quickly learn the key elements of the macOS environment as well as some key shortcuts and tricks?

Many of the technology books currently available are long manuals with very detailed information much of which is not relevant for the end user. These types of books are not ideal for a new user to learn how to use a new system. This book provides new Mac users with a quick guide that covers the key concepts required to start using the new system and all its main features. Not only is it a concise guide that a new user can run through in a few hours but it also includes access to a number of videos that cover most of the material in the book. The over 20 videos provided show the user how the different configuration options and features work in practice. The ideal companion for a practical computer guide!

This guide is based on my personal experience when I migrated from PC to Mac and utilises my experience writing step-by-step technical manuals for tools in the IT/Telecom industry. It will help you through the key points during your transition and walk you through the basics to help you use your Mac efficiently.

What you will learn:

- The key elements of the macOS environment and some of its differences from Windows
- How to configure your laptop to secure it against threats
- How to connect to a network

- How to migrate your Windows files and install Windows (if you really need to...)
- How to set up key functions like e-mail, browser and backup
- Other key functions like application installation/de-installation, storage management and how to recover from failures.
- How to import your photos/media
- Other tips and tricks to use your Mac efficiently

BONUS: exclusive access to over 20 step-by-step videos.
A selection of videos has been created to take you step-by-step through the key parts of this book. To access the video content please check the access instructions at the end of the book in the BONUS MATERIAL section.
Current videos include:

- First steps to configure your Mac
- How to configure your desktop, menu bar, dock and Finder
- How to use tags and smart folders
- How to secure your Mac against threats (user creation and firewall setup)
- How to use Launchpad and Mission Control
- How to configure iCloud and Keychain
- How to configure Safari and set up Time Machine
- How to import data from Windows into macOS and configure:
  - Mac Mail
  - Outlook for Mac
  - Contacts
  - Calendar

Additional videos to cover import of media files (photos/videos), storage management and more will be added during the coming weeks.

TABLE OF CONTENTS

INTRODUCTION

Welcome to the world of Mac! If you are like me you've probably just purchased your first Mac and are looking for a quick guide to teach you how to start using it and how to transfer your data from your old PC.

Five years ago I finally swapped my PC for a Mac. I went home with my new, shiny MacBook Air and when I booted it up I realised that I had no idea how to use it! Where was the file manager? How did I check the space in my hard drive? How did I access my key apps? And, most importantly, how was I to migrate all my data from my old PC to my new Mac? I couldn't even find how to configure Wi-Fi so I could connect to the web and search for instructions on using my new Mac! I had to use my husband's laptop to learn how to configure Wi-Fi and connect to the internet. After that, I used Google to try to find out the key features in my Mac, how to migrate data and where the different settings were etc, but all this took me some time. I thought how much easier it would be to migrate from PC to Mac if I had a straightforward guide to take me through the key steps. I did take a look at some of the books and guides available but what I found were long manuals with in-depth information about the system or guides focusing on specific applications like iTunes and Photos. I just wanted to find out how to set up my Mac, how to use it and how to transfer my data.

As part of the process I started writing this book to help other users like me who were migrating from PC to Mac, and were new to the Mac environment. This book is not meant as an exhaustive guide to macOS but as an introduction, focusing on the key steps that a new user moving from PC to Mac should follow. The initial chapter (Chapter 1) includes a summary of the key steps required for an initial setup, follows with an introduction to the macOS environment (Chapter 2): the Desktop, the Dock, Finder, the Menu Bar, the Trackpad, Siri and other key elements to familiarise yourself with the environment. Chapter 3 includes an overview of some of the key security settings to consider initially: user account set-up, firewall, setting up Gatekeeper, antivirus and using file vault. Chapter 4 explains how to set up Wi-Fi. Chapter 5 explains how to set up iCloud and Keychain to maintain multiple apple devices in sync. Chapter 6 covers e-mail, browser and calendar set up. Chapter 7 goes through data migration, explaining they key data that you need to transfer and how to transfer data between the two systems. Chapter 8 explains the basics of time machine for backup; it also covers the various file format types that can be used to format an external drive to use with your Mac, and drive format compatibility between Windows and macOS. Chapter 9 goes through how to install and de-install applications and also covers some considerations before installing Windows on your Mac. Chapter 10 explains how to import photos and other media. Chapter 11 covers storage management and how to recover from failure, and Chapter 12 runs through some useful information, including frequently used shortcuts, access to special characters, checking disk space, recording, dictation and other useful features. A list of useful links is also included in Chapter 12.

All the information in this book is based on macOS Sierra (10.12). If you are using a different macOS version, some of the paths and screenshots in the book may be different and if your version is older than 10.12 some of the features may not be available, or they may be slightly different.

BONUS: Exclusive access to step-by-step videos covering each part of this book. Instructions on how to access this material can be found in the BONUS section at the end of the book.

CHAPTER 1 - FIRST STEPS

When you change your machine and move from Windows to macOS there are a few key points that can make your transition a lot easier:

1. All your **settings** can be accessed through System Preferences (Apple Menu > System Preferences),which is similar to Control Panel in Windows.

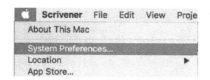

3. **Finder** (first icon on the left on the Dock, the bar at the bottom of your screen) is similar to File Manager in Windows. You can use it to view the drives that are connected to your Mac and all your files and folders.

4. You can access all your **applications** through Launchpad (can be accessed by pressing F4 or through the rocket icon on the Dock).

5. **About this Mac** (Apple Menu > About this Mac) provides you with information about the current version of macOS installed, your display, storage information, disk space management and access to support information.

6. **Shortcuts:** many of the most used Windows shortcuts such as Ctrl + C (copy) and Ctrl + V (paste) work in macOS replacing the Ctrl key in Windows with the Cmd key (⌘) in macOS.

7. The equivalent to **Task Manager** in Windows is "**Activity Monitor**" in macOS . It can be accessed through Finder going to Applications > Utilities or through Launchpad under "Other".

8. The Mac equivalent to Window's Ctrl + Alt + Del is Cmd + Alt + Esc. This shows a pop up window with all open applications and an option to force quit any of the open applications.

9. Most Windows applications have an equivalent application in macOS. For example, MS Office and Photoshop have a macOS version. Hence, in most cases you should be able to continue using the same applications that you are used to in Windows, although you probably need to purchase a separate macOS license. Some applications however do not have a macOS version. In this case, you can either find an application for

macOS that provides similar functionality to that of the Windows version or you can install Windows on your Mac in addition to macOS. Chapter 9 provides additional information and steps to install Windows.

10. **Spotlight** (the magnifying glass at the right hand side of the menu bar on the top of your screen) is a really useful feature. You can type anything in spotlight and it will perform a search on your hard drive and online. It will return applications (so it can be used to search and launch applications), it can also perform unit conversions and be used as a calculator.

Key steps to start using your Mac

This section includes a quick table with the key steps that you need to follow initially to understand the basics and configure your Mac before you start using it. The table includes the key steps of the process with the main actions for each step and links to the different sections where more details are provided. If you are completely new to macOS, I suggest that you run through these steps quickly to set up your Mac before continuing with the rest of the book.

1 - **Security**: set up firewall.	Apple menu>System Preferences>Security & Privacy **General settings:** Select "Require password immediately after sleep or screen saver begins" and "disable automatic login". **Firewall:** in the firewall tab; ensure it's turned on
2 - **Wi-Fi**	Apple menu>System Preferences>Network **Set up your home Wi-Fi**: Select your home Wi-Fi from the drop down menu and when asked, enter your Wi-Fi password. If you don't have a password set up in your Wi-Fi router, you should consider setting one up for security reasons.
3 - **Backup**: Time Machine	Apple menu>System Preferences>time machine **Set up backup**: Connect an external hard drive to store your backups, switch Time Machine on and select the external hard drive as a backup medium. Please note that if the external hard drive defined in Time Machine for back up is not connected, or if this disk is full, Time Machine will not perform a backup.

CHAPTER 2 - GETTING TO KNOW THE ENVIRONMENT

Let's start by going through the main elements of the macOS environment and understanding the various tools and programs that you are likely to use on a day-to-day basis. I will also include my preferred configurations and some tips to configure or customise some of the programs. Explore each setting/ configuration to see what works best for you to make the most out of your Mac.

The Trackpad

The Trackpad is the touch pad that comes built into your Mac. One of the many advantages of a Mac is the functionality of the Trackpad that enables you to access various applications and change screens quickly.

You can configure your Trackpad by going to the Apple menu > System Preferences and selecting "Trackpad". It is worth taking a look at this menu when you first start using your Mac, as it shows you videos of the Trackpad's possible actions and serves as a quick tutorial.

Some of the most useful movements:

- **Right click** by clicking with two fingers on the Trackpad.
- **Scroll** by sliding two fingers across the Trackpad from left to right (horizontal scroll) or up and down (vertical scroll).
- **Switch desktops** by swiping right/left with four fingers.

- **Open mission control** by wiping up with three fingers.

The macOS desktop

After logging into macOS, your desktop will look like the picture below.

Let's have a quick look at the main components of the macOS desktop. It has two main bars, the **menu bar** at the top of the screen and **the dock**, at the bottom. The menu bar includes the apple menu, the menu for the application that is currently active and a number of other icons. The Dock is a bar at the bottom of the screen in macOS that shows your favourite applications as well as any other open applications, documents and the Trashcan. We'll cover both in more detail in later sections, but first let's look at how to customise the desktop.

How to customise the desktop

There are a number of options to customise your desktop; you can change its appearance by selecting and configuring the background image and screen saver, you can select the items you want on the desktop (hard drives, CD drive etc) and you can also re-arrange any files that you are storing on the desktop.

1. To change the **background image** and the **screensaver:** right click on the desktop (click on the Trackpad with two fingers) and select "Change desktop background". This allows you to select from a range of images pre-loaded into your macOS or your own image files. You can also change and configure the screensaver in this window.

2. To organise any files that you are currently storing on your desktop you can:

   • Right click on the desktop and select **Clean up,** which arranges all the icons currently on your desktop by aligning them to a pre-defined grid.

   • Right click on the desktop and select **Sort by** name, kind etc. which orders the icons on the desktop according to the selected criteria.

   • You can also organise your desktop items into **folders**. Right click on the desktop, select "New folder" and drag and drop you files into the folder. You can also select the files that you want to store in a new folder in the desktop while pressing the Cmd key, then right click and select "New folder with selection". This will create a new folder and move all the selected files into it.

3. To select items for your desktop (hard disks, external disks, CDs etc), go to Finder> Preferences, then select General Preferences and select the items you want to see in your desktop.

4. Too many files on the desktop can slow down your system considerably, so try to store your files in your "Documents" folder instead.

The menu bar

The **menu bar** includes a number of drop down menus: the Apple menu, the application menu and other icons.

The **Apple menu** shown below enables access to software updates, the application store, System Preferences, shutdown and others.

The **application menu** is the main menu for the current active application and differs for each application. In the above picture, you can see Finder's application menu (including the following menus: File, Edit, View, Go, Window and Help).

The menu bar also includes a number of additional icons:

1. Quick access to **Time Machine** to enable back-up.

2. A **status bar** with quick information on the status of Wi-Fi, volume and battery.

3. **Active keyboard**: If you have selected at least one keyboard input source in Apple menu > System Preferences > Keyboard, an icon will appear in the menu bar with a flag showing the keyboard currently active. If you

have selected several input sources (for example, British and Spanish) you can click on this icon to switch between the selected keyboards. I use this frequently; it is a very useful icon if you work with multiple languages. This icon will also allow you to open the "Emoji & Symbols" screen where you can select various symbols and characters as well as the "Keyboard Viewer".

4. Access **Airplay** to enable streaming to Airplay-compatible devices (if you have an Airplay device which is active).

5. Access to **Spotlight** which enables quick search of files, folders and the web. You can also use launch applications by typing the application name in Spotlight or you can use it to perform calculations or conversions (for example, typing "5 lbs. in kg." will display the value in kg.)

6. **Messages**, which includes notifications from applications like e-mail, Calendar etc.

7. If you have enabled **fast user switching**, the name of the current user logged in will also appear on the right hand side of the menu bar. You can click on the user name and a drop down will appear with the names of other users; click on one to switch users.

How to configure the menu bar

If you want to maximise the space on your screen for applications, it is possible to hide the menu bar. Go to Apple menu > System Preferences > General and select the option "Automatically hide and show the menu bar".

You can **re-arrange items** in the menu bar by pressing the command key at the same time as the icon and dragging the icon around in the menu bar.

To **remove an item**, press command while selecting the icon and dragging it out of the menu bar.

To **add items** in the menu bar:

1. Open a Finder window.

2. Go to Macintosh HD>System>Library>CoreServices>MenuExtras.

3. You can add any of the additional icons in this folder just by double clicking on the file in finder.

The Dock

The Dock is a bar at the bottom of the screen in macOS that shows your favourite applications as well as any other open applications, documents and the Trashcan.

The above picture shows the default dock configuration for macOS Sierra, including some of the most used applications.

How to customise the Dock

You can change the Dock's appearance and position; you can also change the applications that appear on it, and change their order.

Set up the dock's appearance by going to System Preferences > Dock or by writing "dock" in the spotlight icon on the menu bar (this appears as a search icon).

Some of the **key options** are:

- Size and position of the Dock
- Whether or not items in the Dock are magnified as you scroll over them
- Whether or not the Dock is hidden from view and only appears when the cursor is at the bottom of the screen

I normally have the Dock always showing on the screen, and items on the dock magnified as I scroll over. However, depending on what I am doing, I **hide the Dock** to enable more space on screen for applications. This can be done by selecting "Automatically hide and show the dock" in the above preferences screen.

To **add an application** to the Dock go to Finder > Applications, find the application then drag and drop it into the Dock.

To **remove an application** from the Dock, right click on the application and go to Options > Remove from the Dock.

Right click on any application in the Dock for a number of options, which often include Options > Open at login and Options > Show in Finder.

Finder

Finder allows the user access to applications, drives, folders and files.

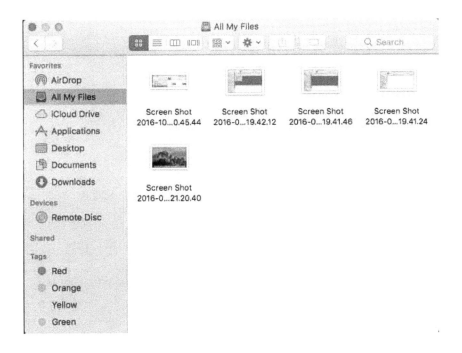

The main Finder window is divided into three key areas: The top bar, the side bar and the main Finder window. The top bar includes a number of icons to select the type of view in the main window, search bar and other actions. The side bar includes key locations in your drive, external devices etc. The main window shows the documents and folders in the location currently selected. Each area is covered in more detail below.

The Sidebar

The **Sidebar** on the left is divided into different sections:

1. **Favourites**: provides access to all applications and main folders like documents, pictures and downloads.

2. **Devices**: enables access to connected drives, DVDs and USBs .

3. **Shared**: enables access to shared services like printers and cloud drives.

4. **Tags**: enables access to colour tags that can be associated with files, applications or folders.

You can add new items to the sidebar by dragging and dropping them on it. For example, you could add a folder that you use frequently into the favourites section.

How to **add your main drive** in finder:

1. Go to Finder > Preferences

2. In the Sidebar tab, select "Hard disks"

You can now see "Macintosh HD" under the devices section on the left hand side in Finder. You can also select other types of devices (DVD/CD drives, external drives etc) to be added to the sidebar.

The top bar

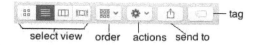

select view   order   actions   send to

The **top bar** provides access to various options:

- The first four icons allow you to select the type of view: icon view, item list or as a screen split vertically or horizontally.

- The order icon allows you to order the items by date, size, tag, type etc.
- The actions icon allows you to select a number of actions for the selected file/s: open, new folder, rename, copy etc.
- The "send to" icon allows you to send the selected file to various applications: Mail, Notes, Messages, Facebook etc.
- The tag icon allows you to assign tags to the selected file/s.

The following section explains how to customise the toolbar in Finder and add additional icons.

How to customise Finder

Go to Finder > Preferences. This opens a new window with a number of tabs:

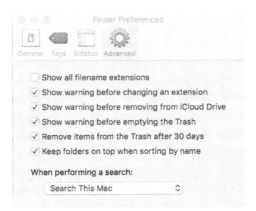

1. **General**: here you can select the drives that appear on your desktop (hard drive, DVD/CD drives, external drives etc), the default directory that opens with a new Finder window and whether folders open in a new tab or window.

2. **Tags:** you can select tags to be shown on the sidebar and also configure

them (add/remove/rename and change tag colour).

3. **Sidebar**: you can select the items that appear on Finder's sidebar.

4. **Advanced**: provides options to display various warnings. For example, a warning before emptying the trash after 30days. You can also define the default location for searches (This Mac/current folder/ last search).

To open a **new Finder window,** go to File > New Finder Window (or Cmd + N). You can also open a **new tab** in the current finder window by going to File > New tab (or Cmd +T). If you have several finder windows open and you want to merge them into one window, you can go to Window > Merge all windows. This will create a separate tab for each open Finder window within a single Finder window.

When you select a folder, by default its contents open in the main window. You can change this behaviour to open them in a new tab. To do this, go to Apple menu > System Preferences > Dock and select your preferred configuration for the option "Prefer tabs when opening documents": "Always", "In full screen only" (default option) or "Manually".

Path Bar and search options

By default Finder does not show you the **Path Bar** of the current folder that you are viewing within Finder. I personally find it quite useful to see the Path Bar, you can enable it by going to View and selecting "Show Path Bar".

When you use search in Finder the default option is to **search** on all the Mac drives and not in the current directory. If you want to change this so that search looks at the current directory only, go to Finder > Preferences and under "Advanced" select "Search the current folder".

How to customise the Finder menu bar

Open a new finder window and click on View > Customise toolbar. A new window appears with a number of icons that you can add to the finder toolbar. You can add icons simply by dragging and dropping them on the Finder toolbar and you can also remove icons by dragging them off the toolbar.

The additional icons that I find most useful are:

1.   **New Folder**: enables you to add a new folder.
3.   **Delete**: deletes the item/s selected.
4.   **Path**: displays the path to the item selected.
5.   **Get info**: provides additional information about the item selected.
6.   **Quick look**: provides a quick preview of the item selected (from macOS Sierra, you can see a preview of a file by selecting the file and clicking on the spacebar).

You can also **add applications, files or folders** to the toolbar:

1.   Find the item you want to add in Finder.
2.   Hold down Cmd as you select the item and drag it to the toolbar.

Once it is in the toolbar, you can **re-organise** the toolbar items by going back to the "**customise toolbar**" menu as indicated above. You can remove icons added to the toolbar by holding down Cmd while dragging and dropping the icon outside the toolbar.

Remember that you can also add items to the Dock, so think about the best way of organising the applications, folders and files that you use often.

Use of tags

Various colour tags appear in the sidebar in Finder. You can use tags to organise your files. For example, you could **rename the default tags** to create different categories; to rename the red tag, select the tag in Finder, right click and select Rename red. You could , for example, rename the tag to "important".

To **associate a tag to a file** or files, right click on the file/s and add the tag that you want to associate with that file. You can associate several tags with the same file. To remove a tag association from a file, right click on the file and select "remove tag...".

In Finder you can automatically **filter all the files with a specific tag** by selecting that tag in the sidebar. You can also search for files with specific tags in Spotlight. For example, typing "tag: important tag: work" in Spotlight would return all the files tagged with both "important" and "work".

If you don't want to use all the default tags and want to remove them from the sidebar, go to Finder > Preferences > Tags tab and select the tags you want to show in Finder.

Smart Folders

Perhaps you use certain specific document searches regularly. For example, if you use tags to categorise your files and keep your receipts in your macOS, perhaps you do a monthly search for all the grocery receipts in the current month. Instead of defining the search each time, you could set up this search using a macOS feature called Smart Folder, which would make the search a lot easier. Smart Folders are "virtual" folders that update automatically following a defined search criteria. You can set up a search including tags, file dates, file names etc.

To create a Smart Folder, in Finder select File > New Smart Folder and define the associated search for the folder:

1.   Make a selection for the search to cover the whole hard drive ("This Mac") or the current folder ("Applications" in the example below).

2. Select the "+" symbol at the top right to add a new search criteria.

3. Choose the criteria to add from the drop down menu. You can select of the type of file, dates (created/modified), name, contents, associated tag/s and many other options.

4. You can repeat steps 2 and 3 to add several search conditions; in the example below I have chosen to search the whole hard drive (This Mac) for files of kind "image" "jpeg" with name matching "wood" and which were modified before a certain date. The results appear in the same window.

5. After creating the smart search you can save it by clicking on the "Save" button and selecting the name and location for the new Smart Folder. A new folder will be created in the selected location.

6. Every time you double click on that folder the search results will be re-calculated and displayed.

Window behaviour

MacOS has three buttons at the top left of each window:

• The red button closes the window.

• The yellow button minimises the window.

- The default function of the green button in macOS is to bring the application into full window mode. You can change this function to maximising the application by pressing the alt key at the same time as hovering over the green button. Clicking and dragging the green button shows the application in split window mode.

Split view

This feature enables you to split the macOS screen in two and show two applications side by side. To enable this:
1. Click and hold the green button in one of the applications
3. Drag the application to one side of the screen.
4. Click on the other application you want to show on split view
To exit split view press "Esc".

Siri

Siri allows you to perform tasks using voice recognition. If you are familiar with Siri on an iPhone or iPad, the same functionality is now available in macOS. One of the uses of Siri is to enable you to multi-task. For example you can write a word document while asking Siri to schedule an appointment in your calendar. Or you could ask Siri to find certain files, write an e-mail, find a contact, do a web search, launch an application and many other tasks. Siri can also control some of your settings: switch Bluetooth or Wi-Fi on/off, increase or decrease the volume and change other settings. I personally find Siri very useful for performing quick tasks while I'm working, for example for a quick web search or to find a contact.

You can start Siri through the icons in the Dock or the menu bar or pressing

Cmd + spacebar a couple of seconds.

You can add the results of any of your Siri searches into the Notification Center by clicking on the + sign on the top right of the Siri results screen:

You can also drag and drop files/images/maps into other windows. For example, if you've asked Siri for a location, you could drop the map that appears on the Siri screen into a calendar appointment.

Launchpad

Launchpad gives you quick access to all applications. You can access it by pressing the F4 key or through the relevant icon on the Dock. By default all applications appear in alphabetical order, but you can re-order them and even organise them into folders.

If the applications don't fit on one screen, Launchpad organises them into multiple screens.

You can also organise selected applications into groups. Drag and drop one icon on top of another and a group will automatically be created.

Mission Control

You can open Mission Control by pressing the F3 key, wiping up with three fingers in the Trackpad or using the Mission Control icon in Launchpad or on the dock. Mission control allows you to organise your applications into several desktops.

Mission Control shows on top of the screen a bar with the different desktops defined. If you have any applications working in full window or split window modes these will also appear in a bar at the top of Mission Control.
The current desktop appears highlighted and all the windows open in that desktop appear on the main part of the screen. This allows you to quickly see the different applications and windows open (minimised windows also appear on screen).

You can add a new desktop space by clicking on the + sign on the bar at the top of the screen and then drag and drop applications into this new space. This can help you to organise your working space, for example, a Desktop space for each purpose. When writing, I have the applications I use frequently open in one Desktop, while I have Finder and Safari open in another.

You can quickly **switch desktops** by swiping right/left with three/four fingers on the Trackpad.

Unfortunately it's not possible to re-name the desktops to identify them, but you can change the background image of each desktop. To do this, you can select the desktop that you want to change and change the background image (Apple menu > System Preferences > Desktop & Screen saver).

If you want an application to always open in a specific desktop, you can define this following these steps:

1. If the application is open, move it to the desired desktop.
2. Make this desktop the active desktop.
3. Right click on the application icon on the dock.
4. Select Options > This desktop.

CHAPTER 3 - HOW TO SECURE YOUR MAC FROM THREATS

This chapter covers the key security settings that you should consider when you first start using your Mac and walks you through the key steps to securing your system:

1. Set up **password protected accounts** for all users and operate a user account without administrator privileges for day-to-day use. Ensure that all accounts are **automatically locked** after a defined period of inactivity.

2. **Switch on Firewall**

3. Set up **Gatekeeper** to allow application downloads from known developers only, or from the Apple Store.

4. Take extra care if you are downloading programs from the internet or from unrecognised developers. Check the source of the file to ensure that it is trustworthy.

5. Always keep your **system up to date** with the latest updates, especially if it contains security enhancements/fixes.

You can change security settings by going to Apple menu>System Preferences>Security & Privacy.

You should also ensure that the administrator account for your home router and Wi-Fi are password protected. This will make it more difficult for hackers to access your home network.

Set up user accounts

To ensure the security and privacy of all the data stored in your Mac you should use personal user accounts. Ideally you should set up one administrator account for your Mac and an account for each user (without administrator rights). Use the administrator account only for administrator activities; operate a separate account for day-to-day use. Most tasks that require administrator permission can be performed entering the administrator username/password without having to log out and log in with the administrator account.

User account creation/settings can be accessed through: Apple menu> System Preferences>Users & Groups

If the lock icon on the bottom left of the window appears as locked, you will need enter your administrator password to unlock this menu.

To **create a new account:**

1.   Click the "+" sign at the bottom left of the window, under the list of existing user names.

2.   A new pop-up window appears, where you can select the type of user.

3.   Enter the full name and account name (if different from full name) and password

4.   Click Create user

Separate user accounts allows each user to configure their own environments and keep their files separate. There are five different user types in macOS:

• **Standard**: standard user account for most of the users. They can make limited changes and only for their own use/account. They cannot see/ change other users' files.

• **Administrator**: this account type has access to all the functionality within your Mac and can create/modify users and change system settings.

• **Managed with parental controls**: usage is limited and managed by the administrator, who can limit web and application usage. Time limits can also be set up for this account type. Parental controls can be set up going to Apple menu> System Preferences>Parental controls.

- **Sharing only**: this type of user can access shared files remotely or share your screen, but is not allowed to log into the Mac. You can enable file or screen sharing under Apple menu > System Preferences > sharing where you can set up the various type/s of sharing allowed and the user/s who have this type of access.

- **Group**: you can set up multiple groups with varying permissions for files/folders. All the users assigned to a group will have the same permissions to access specific files/folders according to the way the group is set up.

- **Guest user**: if this facility is enabled, the account can be used to log into macOS without a password with limited access privileges. This account cannot change any settings or log in remotely. Files created by the guest user are stored temporarily and deleted once the user logs out. If FileVault is active, the guest user only has access to Safari

You can also enable **fast user switching** to quickly toggle between user accounts through an option that appears in the menu bar. To enable this option:

1. Go to Apple menu> System Preferences>Users & Groups
2. Select "Login options" at the bottom left hand side
3. Select "Show fast user switching menu". The name of the current user (or account name/icon as selected) will appear on the menu bar

Ensure that your **account is automatically locked** after a certain period of inactivity. To do this, go to Apple menu>System Preferences>Security & Privacy>General Settings. Select "Require password immediately after sleep or screen saver begins" and also "disable automatic login". You can set the number of minutes of inactivity before the computer **goes to sleep by** going to Apple menu>System Preferences> energy saver. There are alternative power settings for when the laptop is connected to battery or power adaptor.

MacOS firewall

The firewall included within macOS enables you to control the "incoming connections" of applications:

1. **Unlock firewall settings**: Go to Apple menu>System Preferences>Security & Privacy. Select the firewall tab and check the lock icon on the bottom left of the screen. If it's locked, unlock access to firewall settings by clicking on the lock and entering the administrator password.

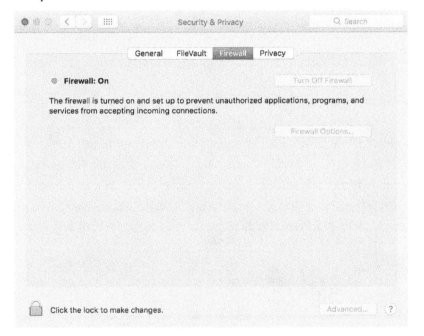

2. **Switch on firewall**: If firewall is off, turn it on clicking on the "Turn on firewall" button.

3. Click on **"Firewall Options"** and:
    *   Select "Automatically allow signed software to receive incoming

connections". This allows software with a valid certificate to be downloaded and installed on your Mac.

•   Select "Enable stealth mode" which will stop your Mac from answering ping and other connection attempts, making it harder for hackers and malware to find your Mac.

•   Once you have selected the first option above, applications with a valid certificate will be configured automatically. If you want to configure application access manually, you can change the current setting for the list of applications in the existing list and also add new applications to the list by clicking on the "+" sign. This will open the applications folder, allowing you to add any currently installed applications to the list.

Gatekeeper

Gatekeeper allows you to control the application that can be installed on your Mac. The safest way to download applications is through the app store, as all applications there have been tested and approved by Apple. You can change Gatekeeper's settings by going to Apple menu>System Preferences>Security & Privacy and selecting General Settings. You can see the options below:

Allow apps downloaded from:
  ◯ Mac App Store
  ◉ Mac App Store and identified developers

Developers can request a developer ID from Apple, so selecting the second option would enable you to install applications from developers with a developer ID.

If you try installing any applications from an unidentified developer with either of the first two settings selected in Gateway, a warning message will appear to indicate that the software is from an unidentified developer. If you are sure that the software is safe and you want to install it, you can open the software package's location in Finder (if you have just downloaded it, it will most likely be in your downloads folder). Right click on the file and select Open. A warning will appear again, but you will be allowed to continue opening the application as long as you have administrator rights (you may be asked to enter your administrator password again).

Antivirus

MacOS includes XProtect, which provides some protection against threats like Trojans. Also, macOS is less susceptible to attack than Windows and is targeted by hackers less, although there have been several cases in the last few years where viruses/malware have affected macOS users. I have run my Mac for years without any antivirus software and I have never had any problems. However, I have recently installed the free version of Avast antivirus (https://www.avast.com/en-gb/mac). Avast is a good free option if you want to install antivirus software. There are also numerous other software packages available that you can purchase for macOS. The same antivirus software available for Windows is normally also available for macOS. For example, Norton, McAfee and Panda have macOS versions.

FileVault

FileVault enables hard drive encryption. This is a good feature if you have sensitive data on your hard drive that you don't want anyone to access. However, please note that if you lose your password and the FileVault security key, all data on your hard drive will be lost, so please use this feature with care. You can enable FileVault by going to Apple menu>System

Preferences>Security & Privacy and selecting the FileVault tab.

Set up automatic updates

It is important to keep your macOS software up to date with updates, especially ones that include security updates/new features. You can set up automatic updates under Apple menu>System Preferences>App Store

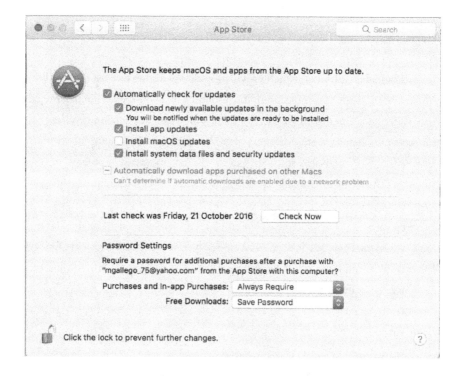

I recommend that you select "Install system data files and security updates" to ensure that any security updates provided by Apple are updated automatically. The other options are:

1. Download available updates in the background: macOS updates will be downloaded in the background if you click this option. This will apply also to main system updates like a new version of macOS like macOS Sierra. You will be notified when new updates are available to install.

2. Install application updates: will automatically install updates of applications downloaded using App Store.

3. Install macOS updates. If this is selected, system updates will be updated automatically. This does not apply to major system upgrades like macOS Sierra. For major upgrades you will still be asked if you want to install the upgrade.

CHAPTER 4 - CONNECTING TO THE WEB

If you are connecting your Mac directly to your router, you should be able to just connect the cable and access the internet without having to perform any specific configuration. Nowadays, however, most users connect to the web through a wireless router.

Wi-Fi

If you are connecting to the internet using a wireless router you will need to configure Wi-Fi in your Mac. To do this you need to know your Wi-Fi's network name or SSID and network key or password. If you don't know these details, you can check them by connecting to your Wi-Fi router (in many cases these details appear also on a sticker on the back of the router).

To configure Wi-Fi:

1.   Go to Apple menu> System Preferences>Network.

2.   Select Wi-Fi

3.   In the network name drop down menu you can see a list of the network names that your Mac is currently receiving. Select your Wi-Fi's network name.

4.   Enter your Wi-Fi's network password in the new pop-up window.

5.   Select "Remember this network".

6.   Select "Apply" in the main window.

7.   The Wi-Fi icon in the menu bar shows the current status of the Wi-Fi connection. Right click the icon to see more details, as well as other

available Wi-Fi networks.

The Wi-Fi icon on the menu bar shows the current status of the Wi-Fi connection. You can click on the icon to switch Wi-Fi on/off, to see which networks are available, join a network or open network preferences. The network that we are currently connected to will appear with a √ sign next to it.

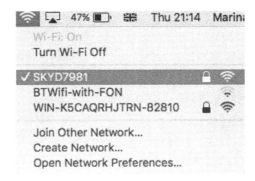

CHAPTER 5 - SETTING UP ICLOUD AND KEYCHAIN

This chapter covers how to set up iCloud and keychain. To be able to set up both of them you first need to have an **apple/icloud ID**. Normally this is set up for you when your computer is first configured if you buy it directly from an apple store. However, if you don't have an apple ID, you can request one going to the following web: http://www.icloud.com. You can then click on "Don't have an apple ID? Create yours now" at the bottom of the screen. You then need to enter one of your existing e-mail addresses which will be your new apple ID and some personal details requested to create your new account.

iCloud

iCloud enables you to store data from multiple applications in the apple Cloud as well as share data among multiple Apple devices.
To **set up** iCloud:
1.   Go to Apple menu> System Preferences>iCloud
2.   Login with your apple ID
3.   You can now select the services that you want to enable for iCloud. The following services are available through iCloud:
   • **iCloud drive**: allows you to save files in the iCloud so that they can be available to any device (Mac, iPhone or iPad). You can share specific files by storing them on the iCloud drive in Finder; files stored in your iCloud folder can be updated from multiple devices. You can also set up your Documents folder and your Desktop to be

stored on your iCloud. This can be configured in the Storage management features (Apple menu > About this Mac > Storage > Manage)

- **Share and store data from multiple applications**: Photos, Mail, Calendar, Safari, Notes, Keychain etc. You can set up the applications that you want to be active on iCloud.
- **Back to my Mac**: this feature allows you to configure your Mac to be accessed remotely. It allows remote file and screen sharing. To use this feature you need at least two Macs.
- **Find my Mac**: this feature can help you find your Mac if it's lost or stolen. The application will display your Mac's location on a map or start a chime on your Mac. You can also remotely lock or erase your Mac using this feature. You can access "Find my Mac" either

through your iCloud account on the web, or if you have an iPhone or iPad you can download the app.

I use my iCloud storage for the data that I want to share between my Apple devices (mainly my iPhone and my Mac). I currently have iCloud active for Keychain (password storage), Safari (bookmarks, history etc), contacts, reminders, Calendars and Notes. I also have "Find my Mac" active.

You should consider how you want to manage your data storage/sharing, and how you want to use your iCloud account. Take into account that Apple only provides free iCloud storage of up to 5GB. Once you have used 5GB you will need to upgrade your subscription. Apple offers various options to **upgrade your storage space**. To check these options, go to "Manage" in the bottom right corner of the iCloud preferences window and click "buy more storage". You can upgrade (and downgrade) your storage plan through this window.

If you want to store your photos on iCloud or use the space management features to save Documents and Desktop files on iCloud you will most likely need more than 5GB in the short/medium term.

You can also enable **Family Sharing** if you have several family members using one or several Apple devices. This allows all the members of the family group to share purchases, and pay with a single credit card, and it allows parents to approve kids' purchases. To do this:

1. Go to Apple menu> System Preferences>iCloud

2. Select "Set up family"

3. Follow the on-screen instructions.

4. Once you have created a family group, you can invite members of your family to join:

5. Go to Apple menu > System Preferences > iCloud > Family > Add Family Member.

6. Type the name or e-mail address of the family member you want to invite.

7. Follow the on-screen instructions.

Keychain

Nowadays we have so many different logins with differing password requirements that we need to remember (or write down) many different username and password combinations. I personally find it impossible to remember all of them. I used to store all my password information in a password manager app, which, despite being a relatively secure option, was not very user friendly. That is why I love Keychain, it enables you to store all your application passwords and enter them automatically, resulting in seamless logins to multiple websites. Keychain also allows you to share login and password information across all your Apple devices (MacBook, iPhone and iPad). Keychain can store data that you may want to keep secure like PINs and credit card information. If, like me, you struggle to remember all your passwords then Keychain can make your life a lot easier. However, it mainly works with Safari, so if you prefer other internet browsers you will not be able to use Keychain, although Firefox has a plugin for Keychain (http://addons.mozilla.org/en-GB/firefox/addon/keychain-services-integration/) that you can try. I have chosen to use Safari to make the most of Keychain across my Apple devices.

You can **enable Keychain** under iCloud preferences:
1.   Go to Apple menu> System Preferences>iCloud
2.   Login with your apple ID
3.   Select "Keychain" to enable it

You can enable Keychain in all your other apple devices and share the Keychain data among them.

If you want Keychain to **autofill usernames and passwords,** make sure that this option is set up, go to Safari > Preferences > Passwords and make sure that the option "Autofill user names and passwords" is selected.

To add the **Keychain icon to the menu bar**:
1.   Start Keychain access going to Finder > Applications > Utilities >

Keychain access (or typing Keychain access in spotlight).

2.   In the menu bar, go to Keychain access > Preferences.

3.   Under General, click "Show keychain status on the menu bar".

A lock icon appears for Keychain that will allow you quick access to lock your keychains. You can also open Keychain access quickly through this icon. **Keychain access** is an application that stores all your keychain data and enables you to change your keychain configuration and security features. You can also access keychain access through Applications > Utilities > Keychain access or typing "Keychain Access" on spotlight.

When you open Keychain access you can see all your keychains on the navigation pane on the left hand side and the data stored in the selected keychain in the main pane. You can double-click on an entry to open it and click "Show password" to see the password for that entry. You will be asked to enter that keychain's password before the password appears on screen.

By default, your login Keychain (which is the default keychain) is unlocked every time you log in. If you are storing sensitive information in keychain, you can set up a separate keychain that will have to be unlocked manually. You can set up multiple Keychains with different levels of security. For example, you can use your login keychain for less sensitive items that you may use often and create a second Keychain that requires a password to be unlocked and is locked automatically when the screen sleeps.

To **create a new Keychain**:

1. Open Keychain access (using the icon on the menu bar or type keychain access in spotlight).
2. Go to File > New Keychain.
3. Create a new Keychain and enter a password to protect it.

To change the **security level of an existing keychain**:

1. Select the keychain.
2. Right click and select "Change settings for keychain xxx"
3. You can set the security settings for a keychain to lock after a certain number of minutes of inactivity and/or when sleeping.

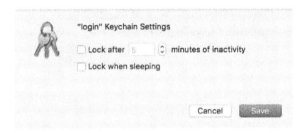

CHAPTER 6 - SETTING UP E-MAIL AND BROWSER

This chapter covers the key settings that you can change in Safari, macOS's default web browser and how to set up an e-mail account in both Mail for macOS and Outlook for macOS. I have also included some details about macOS's Calendar application. I personally use Calendar and I think that it has some really good features. I have included a summary here to help you make a choice between Calendar and other calendar applications.

Web browsing

The default browser in macOS is Safari. If you prefer to use a different browser, you can download one from the internet (Firefox, Chrome, Opera, Netscape, Internet Explorer etc). However, you need to take into account that there are some macOS built in features that allow you to easily store and share data among multiple apple devices that you may not be able to use if you decide to use a different browser. For example, Keychain and sharing of browser history and bookmarks across multiple Apple devices.

After installing your chosen browser, you can import your bookmarks. To do this, you first need to export the bookmarks from your PC browser. The steps to do this depend on the browser and version and hence are not detailed here. The steps to import your bookmarks into Safari are detailed in the following section.

Safari

To **change the default search engine and homepage:**

1. Go to Safari > Preferences
2. In the General tab, you can select the search engine from the drop down menu and type in the page that you want to set up as your homepage.

Migration Assistant can help you import your bookmarks. It is also possible to import them manually into Safari. To do this, you need to first export them into html format in Windows (the steps will depend on the browser that you use in Windows). Then to **import the bookmarks** in Safari, open Safari and go to File > Import from > Bookmarks html file

E-mail set up

This section covers the key steps required to set up your e-mail account/s in both Mail and MS Outlook for macOS. It also covers how to import your contacts into the Contacts application on your Mac.

Activate and set up your Apple e-mail account

When you sign up for an Apple account, you get a free iCloud account. You can see the details of your iCloud account within your Apple id's page:

1. Go to https://appleid.apple.com/
2. Enter your login details
3. Under the "account" area you can find your iCloud e-mail address

To activate it you just need to set up iCloud (see chapter 5) and your Apple e-mail account will be configured automatically and added within the mail application in macOS

Set up macOS Mail

Open Mail by clicking on the Mail icon on the dock and go to Mail>Accounts. The **setup** is quite straightforward for most of the common e-mail services like Yahoo and Google: Select the type of e-mail that you want to configure and enter your e-mail address and password.

You can **import** the data from an external mailbox or from an mbox file, open Mail and go to File>Import mailboxes.

If you were using MS Outlook in your PC, you will need to convert the pst file created by MS Outlook into Mbox format to import the data into Mail. To perform this conversion you can install Mozilla's Thunderbird (http:// www.mozilla.org/en-GB/thunderbird/) free e-mail software on your Windows machine and then open the pst file. Thunderbird will then create the mbox file that you can then use to open in Mac's Mail program; you can find some instructions here: www.techwalla.com/articles/how-to-convert-pst-to-mbox. You can also use the outlook_converter_wizard (http:// gallery.technet.microsoft.com/Convert-PST-to-MBOX-25f4bb0e) which is a Windows application to convert pst files to mbox. There are also numerous paid applications that convert from .pst to .mbox. Once you have the data in .mbox format:

Once you have the data in mbox format:

1. Open Mail and go to File >Import Mailboxes

2. Select Files in Mbox format.

3. Select the Mbox file to import and select Choose.

4. The file will be imported into Mail and will appear in the left hand pane.

Set up MS Outlook for macOS

To configure Outlook for macOS open Outlook, go to Outlook>Preferences and select "Accounts". Click on the "+" sign to add a new account and select the type of account (Exchange, other e-mail or directory service). For a Yahoo/

Gmail or similar account, you need to select other e-mail and add the e-mail address and password. Outlook will automatically set up the account and import all your e-mails.

If you want to import mail from your PC's MS Outlook, you can export the mail into a .pst file in your PC and then import this file into MS Outlook for macOS. To do this, follow the steps below:

Go to File>Import and select Import from Outlook data file (.pst or .olm).

In the next screen, select the file type Outlook for Windows data file (.pst).

Find and select the .pst file to be imported.

It is not possible to open .msg files from Outlook for Windows in your Outlook for macOS. To view a .msg file in macOS you can either use an external application or include the .msg file/s in a .pst file and then follow the steps indicated above to import the .pst file into Outlook for macOS.

One of the applications that allows you to open .msg files in your macOS is Msgviewer (http://sourceforge.net/projects/msgviewer/). You can drag and drop .msg files into the free application, see the content of the file and save it. You can also open and save any attachments. I use it when I want to open a .msg file from Outlook for Windows, I find it easy to use and effective.

Import Outlook contacts from Windows into the Contacts application in macOS

Follow these steps to import your contacts into macOS's Contacts application:

1. Export your Outlook contacts into .txt files.
2. Copy the exported .txt files to your Mac.
3. Open the Contacts application in macOS.
4. Within Contacts, go to File>Import.
5. Select the .txt file/s to be imported.

Calendar

MacOS's Calendar app, has a number of useful features apart from the usual calendar functionality to create appointments, reminders etc., you can:

1. **Define and synchronise multiple calendars**: for example, separate personal and work calendars. You can also synch calendars from external accounts like Yahoo, Google etc. You can choose how to display each calendar; display them all in one view or display only one, or view several of the available calendars by selecting them from the calendars pane on the left hand side. You can display the calendar pane by clicking on "calendars".

2. **Birthdays and holidays**: Birthdays are imported automatically from contacts and there is a built-in local holidays calendar, so you can see the public holidays in the UK for example. You can switch on the birthdays and local holidays calendars within the preferences window in Calendar, by going to Calendar > Preferences and then going to the "General" tab.

3. **iCloud sharing**: You can set up iCloud to work with Calendar so that you can share your Calendar among various Apple devices like your Mac, iPad and iPhone. You can also share your Calendar with other people or make it a public calendar which is available online. (See details below)

Setting up iCloud calendar

You can set up your iCloud calendar following these steps:

1. Go to Calendar > Preferences > Accounts tab
2. Select the iCloud icon on the left hand side
3. Select "Enable this account" and enter your iCloud e-mail address in the "User name" field if it does not already appear there.
4. Then select how often you want to refresh the Calendar or set it to "push" which means that every time a new event is available it will be automatically updated.

Sharing your Calendar

To share your Calendar, activate the Calendars pane and select the Calendar you want to share. Right click and select "Share Calendar". You can then select whether to share this Calendar with one or several of your contacts and also to share it online:

1. Type in contact names and their details will be displayed automatically.

2. Select to give them access to view only or to view and edit.

3. To share it online, mark it as "Public Calendar". macOS will assign your calendar a URL that you can then share via Facebook, e-mail etc (options to share the URL appear in the same window by clicking the button next to the URL).

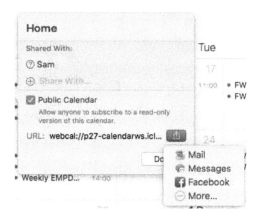

Adding and editing new appointments

To add a new event you can:

1. Click the "+" sign next to the Calendars button. This allows you to create a quick event. For example, you could type "Lunch on Monday at 17:00" and Calendar will automatically schedule this in the calendar.

2. You can double click on a date in the calendar. This will open the Event Inspector window and enable you to create a new event on that date.

If you add a location, Calendar will show a small map of that location that can be expanded by clicking on it (directions and travel time from current location will also be shown if Calendar has been allowed to use current location. This can be set up for each application under System Preferences > Security & Privacy > Privacy tab). Calendar also shows the current weather at the event location.

CHAPTER 7 - MIGRATING YOUR FILES FROM WINDOWS

The aim of this chapter is to help the user migrate the key data from Windows to macOS. A migration assistant is available in macOS that can automatically migrate some of the data from Windows like e-mail, browser info, Calendar and some files and folders. You can also migrate your data manually. This chapter covers both the manual migration and the use of migration assistant.

How to migrate your files

Most data types that you normally use in Windows can be read by macOS too, for example image/video/mp3 files, text/word processor files, html files etc. MS Office files are generally compatible with both Windows and macOS as long as you have MS Office for macOS (.msg files need to be included in a .pst file to be recognised in Outlook for macOS) and bookmarks can be manually exported from your Windows browser and imported in macOS.

If you want to copy the data manually, you can use an external hard drive to copy the files that need to be transferred. Your Mac should be able to read files from any Windows formatted hard drive or external memory device, although it may not be able to write to it, depending on the device's type of format (for more information on formatting types, go to the section External disk format, in chapter 8). The following sections cover the key data types that you would normally need to import: bookmarks, e-mail, calendar and contacts.

Any files (for example, files from your **Desktop and in your Documents folder) or media files** (photos, videos, music etc) that you want to migrate can be copied from your PC and moved into your Mac directly using a USB stick or an external hard drive.

Bookmarks

Bookmarks from your Windows web browser (for example, Netscape or Internet Explorer) can be exported from your Windows browser and imported into your Mac browser. If you are going to use **Safari**, you can import any bookmarks exported previously into an html file by going to File > Import from > Bookmarks html file. The process to export your bookmarks from Windows will depend on your browser type and version, hence it's not covered here but you should see an option to export bookmarks (in many cases either under the File or Bookmarks menu).

E-mail, Calendar and contact information

Before you start importing your e-mail, calendar and contact information to your new Mac you need to decide which application/s you are going to use. In this section I am going to cover importing data to macOS's applications: Mail, Calendar and Contacts; and also importing into MS Outlook for macOS.
To be able to import your files into macOS you first need to export the files from your current e-mail application in Windows. I have not detailed the steps to export your e-mail data from Windows as these steps will be different depending on the application and the version of this application that you are using in Windows. If you are not sure how to export your data, you can run a quick search on the web to find the detailed steps to follow. The data format that you need to import the data into macOS will also depend on the e-mail application that you are going to use in macOS. I have included two sections

below, the first one explains how to import your data into macOS's Mail, Calendar and Contacts applications and the second one how to import into Outlook for macOS.

Import Outlook contacts from Windows into the Contacts application in macOS

MacOS's Mail: The Mail application in macOS can import data from Netscape, Eudora and Thunderbird as well as being able to import e-mail in .mbox format. If you were using MS Outlook in Windows you will have to first create a .pst file in Outlook and convert it later to .mbox. Conversion from .pst to .mbox format is not straight forward as .pst is a Microsoft proprietary format. To perform this conversion you can install Mozilla's Thunderbird (http://www.mozilla.org/en-GB/thunderbird/) free e-mail software on your Windows machine and then open the .pst file. Thunderbird will then create the .mbox file that you can use to open in Mac's Mail program; you can find some instructions here: www.techwalla.com/articles/how-to-convert-pst-to-mbox. You can also use the outlook_converter_wizard (http://gallery.technet.microsoft.com/Convert-PST-to-MBOX-25f4bb0e) which is a Windows application to convert .pst files to .mbox. There are also numerous paid applications that convert from .pst to .mbox. Once you have the data in .mbox format:

1. Open Mail and go to File >Import Mailboxes
2. Select "Files in Mbox format".
3. Select the Mbox file to import and select "Choose".
4. The file will be imported into Mail and will appear in the left hand pane.

Calendar: You can export your **calendar** items into **.ics format** to import them into the **Calendar application** on your Mac. **To import to macOS's Calendar app**, open Calendar and go to File > Import. Select the .ics file to import and when asked, select the calendar into which you want to import the calendar items. If you want to import into a new calendar you will need to create a new calendar before importing the data (File > New calendar).

Contacts: You need to first export your contacts in Windows into a .txt file. To import the contacts into Contacts for macOS follow these steps:

1. Copy the exported .txt files to your Mac.

2. Open the Contacts application in macOS.

3. Within Contacts, go to File>Import.

4. Select the .txt file/s to be imported.

Importing into Outlook for macOS

E-mail: If you are planning to use MS Outlook for macOS, you will need a .pst file which can be exported directly from MS Outlook for Windows. To import a .pst file into Outlook for Mac go to File > Import and select "Outlook data file".

Calendar: You can export your calendar items into **.ics forma**t and then import them into **MS Outlook for macOS** . To import the contacts, open MS Outlook and select the calendar in the left hand pane. Then open Finder, find the .ics file and drag and drop it into Outlook.

Contacts: You can export your contacts from **MS Outlook** in Windows into a **.csv file**, which can then be imported into **MS Outlook for macOS** by going to File > Import. Select "Contacts or messages from a text file" and then "Import contacts from a tab - or comma - delimited text file". Then select the file to import. To import your contacts into the Contacts application in macOS, open the application and create a new group (File>New group). The new group will appear on the left pane in Contacts. Select the new group and go to File > Import. Select the .txt file to import and click Open.

Using Migration Assistant

MacOS has a built in Migration Assistant that will help you to migrate your data from another Mac or PC. To start the Migration Assistant, go to Launchpad > Other > Migration Assistant, or Finder > Applications >Utilities >Migration Assistant. It will walk you through the steps required to transfer the data.
To transfer the data both your PC and Mac need to be connected to the same Wi-Fi or Ethernet network. To migrate from a PC you will also have to download the PC Migration Assistant (http://support.apple.com/kb/DL1557) on your PC. The link to download this is provided by Migration Assistant (www.apple.com/migrate-to-mac).
Migration Assistant will enable you to migrate the following information:
- E-mail, contacts and calendar information.
- Bookmarks
- iTunes data
- Images
- Settings like the background photo, browser homepage and other files and folders.

Please note that the data is only copied from the user logged in the PC to the user logged on to macOS. If you want to transfer data for several users you need to repeat the migration with each user logged in.
Migration Assistant can be used at any time and can also be used to migrate data between two Macs.

CHAPTER 8 - HOW TO SET UP BACKUP

To be able to perform a backup with your Mac you first need to connect an external hard drive. If you are using the hard drive for macOS only you can just use a hard drive with HFS format. However, if you are going to use the hard drive for both Window and macOS then you need to consider which file system is best for your needs. This is why I have included in this section a summary of the different file systems, their advantages and disadvantages.

Storage file systems

When I first got my Mac I had to do some research to understand why, depending on the selected drive, I could only read it, or read and write to it. I think that it is important at least to have a basic understanding of the various file systems. There are a number of different data formats to consider when you format an external hard drive to use with your Mac. The best format for an external hard drive/memory stick will depend on your intended use of the drive. If you are only going to use the drive with your Mac you should format it as macOS Extended (journaled), which is the most reliable option. However, a Windows system will not be able to read this format.
If you want to read and write to a hard drive from both Windows and macOS the best file format to use is exFAT. You could also use FAT32 but this file format has a number of limitations like file size and maximum disk partition

size (see below). FAT and ExFAT allow read and write access in both Windows and macOS.

NTFS is the Windows native file system and any hard drive that you have been using with Windows is likely to be formatted with NTFS. It allows read and write access in Windows and read access in macOS, so your Mac will be able to read any drive that you have previously used with Windows. To write to an NTFS drive in macOS you need to install additional drivers (there are free drivers available for this, see below for more information).

You can format a drive as FAT, ExFAT or macOS Extended (journaled) using the Disk Utility in your Mac. Detailed steps are provided in the next section. To format a drive in NTFS you need to use a Windows machine or a specific driver like NTFS 3G, Tuxera or Paragon as mentioned below.

You can find some more details of each file system below:

FAT32

FAT32 is an old file system but one of the most widely supported.

Advantage: Both Windows and macOS can read and write to FAT32.

Limitations:

1. Files cannot be bigger than 4GB. This should not affect the majority of files, but could affect, for example, some large video files.
2. Disk partition cannot be bigger than 32GB.

ExFAT

Advantages:

1. ExFAT drives can also be read and written to in both Windows and macOS.
2. ExFAT is optimised for flash drives and allows a bigger file size than FAT32 as well as allowing volumes bigger than 32GB. If your external

hard drive is over 32GB or you are going to store big files like, for example, video recordings, you can use the ExFAT format to avoid FAT32 limitations.

Disadvantages: Lacks security features and is less reliable than macOS Extended.

NTFS

NTFS is a proprietary Microsoft format and is the default format for most Windows systems.

Advantages: Windows can read and write NTFS.

Disadvantages: macOS systems can read NTFS but not write it. To write to an NTFS drive you will need to download NTFS-3G (http://www.tuxera.com/community/open-source-ntfs-3g/), which is a free (open source) third party driver for macOS. There are other options like Paragon (http://www.paragon-software.com/home/ntfs-mac/index.html) or Tuxera (www.tuxera.com/products/tuxera-ntfs-for-mac/), which provide NTFS support for macOS for around £20.

HFS (Hierarchical File System or macOS Extended)

This is the native format for macOS and the most reliable option for your Mac. HFS includes journaling as an option. Journaled systems provide better reliability and are easier to repair than non-journaled systems, hence they are preferred for external hard drives that are more likely to become corrupted.

How to format a hard drive

To format a hard drive, use Disk Utility (Applications > Utilities > Disk Utility) following these steps:

1. Select the hard drive that you want to format in the left pane.

2. Select "Erase". A new pop up window will open.

3. Select the format type from the following options:
   - MacOS Extended (journaled)
   - MacOS Extended (Case sensitive, journaled)
   - MS-DOS (FAT)
   - ExFAT

4. Click "Erase"

If you want to format a drive using NTFS you can either format the drive using an application like Tuxera NTFS or Paragon NTFS, or you can format the drive using Windows.

How to set up backup

Time Machine enables you to back up the contents of your Mac's hard drive. For automatic backups, open Time Machine and select the hard drive to back up to. You will need an external device on which to store your backup data and you can choose whether or not you want to encrypt your back ups. In the Time Machine options menu you can also select the files and directories to exclude from back up. After the first full backup, time machine will create hourly backups of any files that have changed, providing the backup drive is connected.

You can start a backup manually by right clicking on the Time Machine icon on the menu bar and selecting "Back up now".

To **set up** Time Machine:

1. Click the Time Machine icon on your Desktop bar > open Time Machine preferences or go to the Apple menu>System Preferences>Time Machine.

2. Click on the Options button to set up the following:

- Back up location/drive.
- Select the directories that will be excluded from your backups.

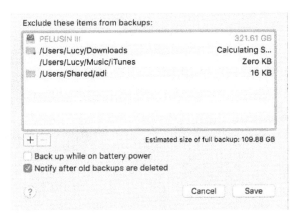

3. If the Time Machine icon does not appear in your menu bar you can enable it in this screen (the option is at the bottom of the screen, next to the options button).

Please note that if the backup drive selected during Time Machine setup is not connected or is full, no back up will be performed. Ensure that you connect your backup drive regularly and that it has enough space for the backup. If you don't have this drive permanently connected to your Mac, you can start a manual back up when the drive is connected by selecting the Time Machine icon in the menu bar and selecting "Back up now".

To **restore** a file/directory/application from backup:

1. Enter Time Machine either through the icon on your menu bar, or by selecting enter Time Machine.

2. Time Machine displays the dates of the different backups available for restore on the right hand side. You can search for specific files or folders in the main window and see the versions available in the different backups.

3. Choose one and click restore.

To perform a **full restore** of the whole systems from Time Machine you need to access macOS Utilities. To do this, press Cmd + R as soon as the laptop re-starts (hold for a few seconds until you see the Apple appear on screen). This will launch macOS Utilities which includes an option to perform a full restore. Time Machine keeps hourly backups for the last 24h, daily backups for the last month and weekly backups for as long as the space in the backup drive will allow. Once the backup drive starts running out of space, Time Machine starts deleting old backups.

CHAPTER 9 - APPLICATION INSTALLATION

This section provides a quick overview on how to install and de-install applications in macOS, including those applications that are not allowed by Gatekeeper. It also provides an overview of the different options that you need to consider to install Windows on your Mac.

How to install and de-install an application

You can **install** applications in macOS from the App Store or by downloading them from the internet:

1. To download an application from the App store, click on the App Store on the Dock to open it, then select the application, click install and click "Open" to run the application. The application will automatically be added to your Applications folder.

2. If you download the application from the internet, files are normally downloaded as DMG file. Double click on the DMG file and follow the instructions. In many occasions you will need to drag and drop the "unpackaged" application into the "Applications" area in Finder (this will be clearly indicated on screen).

3. If the application is not from the App store or it is not from an "identified" developer, macOS will not allow you to open the file for security reasons. Apps from the App store or from identified developers have been checked by Apple. If you download and install a file that has not been verified by Apple there is a risk that the application could

contain some malware. Quite a few applications are part of this category. If you are confident that the application is safe, follow the steps below to install it. If you are not sure, I recommend that you do a bit of research on the application to ensure that is safe before you install it. To install an application from outside the App store that is not from an identified developer:

    3.1.   Download the application

    3.2.   Open Finder and select the Downloads folder.

    3.3.   Right click on the application downloaded and select Open. A warning will appear.

    3.4.   Click Open. You may be asked to enter your administrator password.

To **uninstall** an application, right click on it in the Applications folder in Finder and select "Move to trash" or just drag and drop the application into the trash.

Do you need to install Windows on your Mac?

Although most programs are now available for both Windows and macOS, there are still some apps that only run on Windows. For those, you have two main options to run Windows on your Mac; the first is to create a separate partition for Windows and have a full Windows installation. The second option is to run virtual machine software in macOS that allows you to run Windows.

I used to have a separate partition with Windows on my Mac. I found the installation process really easy through Boot Camp Assistant and I had no problems running Windows on my Mac, although I only used it a handful of times. For me, there are two key drawbacks to this approach; the first one is that you need to restart every time you want to swap between macOS and Windows, which can be quite annoying. The second drawback is that the Windows partition eats quite a lot of space in your hard drive. For me the use of Windows for one or two apps once in a while did not justify the amount of disk space that

I was losing to the Windows partition, so I uninstalled Windows. The uninstall process is equally easy using Boot Camp Assistant, which also re-partitions the space previously occupied by Windows.

I have not tried the option to run a virtual machine as I have not really felt the need to run Windows again, but there are quite a few options available. If you are only running Windows applications that do not require a lot of processing power you can try this option before giving up space on your hard drive for a full Windows partition. You can try VirtualBox (http://www.virtualbox.org) which is Open Source and hence free, Parallels (http://www.parallels.com/uk/products/desktop/) which has a trial period of 14 days or other paid software like VMWare (http://store.vmware.com/store/vmwde/en_GB/DisplayProductDetailsPage/ThemeID.29219600/productID.323416600). (There are many other virtual machine applications, I have just listed a few options).

How to install Windows with Boot Camp Assistant

If you decide to install a full version of Windows on your hard drive alongside macOS, Boot Camp Assistant will walk you through all the steps required to partition your hard drive and install Windows. Before installing Windows, you will need:

1.   A copy of Windows 7 or later.
2.   At least 55GB of available space in your Mac.
3.   A USB drive or external hard drive with at least 16GB free space for most Mac versions (see Apple's support page: http://support.apple.com/en-gb/HT201468 for full details). Boot Camp will use this to install Windows.

You can launch Boot Camp Assistant by typing "Boot Camp Assistant" in Spotlight.

To switch between macOS and Windows you will need to restart your Mac. While you are restarting, press the alt key (alt ⌥) during the initial white screen to access the Boot Camp menu, which enables you to choose between the two partitions for boot up (macOS or Windows).

CHAPTER 10 - HOW TO IMPORT PHOTOS/MEDIA

When you connect your phone or an external memory card to your Mac, Photos
will automatically be displayed along with some options to import your pictures
into Photos' Library. Photos is macOS's application to store, organise, view and
edit your photos and videos. It provides some good features to help organise
your photos; it automatically detects faces and groups pictures by location and
date as well as automatically creating albums. Photos makes it very easy to store
and organise your files. However, if you normally use more advanced photo
editing software like Photoshop or Gimp then you will find that once your
photos are stored in Photos' internal library it is really difficult to export them to
use in external tools. The following section provides a quick summary of the
pros and cons of importing your photos directly into Photos' library.

If you are going to use Photos to manage your files, you can turn on iCloud
Photo library so that all your files are stored in the cloud and can be accessed
from all your Apple devices (Mac, iPhone, iPad etc). To switch on iCloud Photo
Library, go to Apple menu > System Preferences > iCloud and make sure that
Photos is selected on the right hand side. Before moving all your photos to the
cloud you need to consider the amount of space that you are likely to need in the
cloud, and the fact that Apple only provides 5GB of free space, which is
unlikely to be enough to store all your photos. This means that if you want to
store your photos on the cloud you will probably have to upgrade your iCloud
plan.

Managed vs. Referenced photo files

When you think about importing your photos/media from your camera/iPhone/ iPad into your Mac you need to consider how you want to store them. You can either download all the files into a specific location in your hard drive/external hard drive (referenced photo files) or import the files into a library within macOS's Photos application (managed photos). The key advantage of managed photos is that all the files are stored within the same location, making it very easy to store and back up, so this is a very quick and easy method of managing your photos. The two key disadvantages are:

1.   You need a lot of space for the Photos Library. Using referenced photos allows you to store the files in external hard drives that you can connect/ disconnect as required.

2.   Once the files have been imported into the library, it's not easy to export the files again to use them in other photo editing/management apps.

For those reasons I prefer to manage my own photo storage and use referenced files. However, in this case you need to manage the storage and backup of files yourself. Even if a photo appears within Photos, if the original file is lost you will not be able to access that photo.

If you are likely to want to access the original image files to use them in a separate program you should reference your files but if you are not likely to need external access to them you can make the workflow easier by using Photos to store your files.

The option to select either manage or reference your photo files can be found in Photos > Preferences. The following window shows the Preferences window within Photos:

The setting under Importing allows you to choose when you import a file into Photos whether you want a copy of that file stored within the Photos Library (imported photos are called managed photos) or whether you want to keep the file outside of Photos (referenced photos).

How to select the program that opens when a device/card is connected

By default, Photos opens automatically when you connect an external device/card. To stop Photos from opening automatically, follow these steps:

1. Connect the device. Photos will open automatically and you will see the device name at the top left (for example, Marina's iPhone).

2. De-select the option "Open Photos for this device" that appears next to the device name. Please note that this option is device-specific, so when you connect a different device or card Photos will still open automatically.

You can follow these steps for each device/card.

This will stop Photos from opening automatically each time you connect the device but you need to either select an alternative application to automatically open when you connect your iPhone, or manually upload the photos to your Mac.

I use Image Capture to import my photos, I have it set up to launch automatically when I connect the phone as I only connect in order to download photos/media and to back up. To set up Image Capture to open automatically:

1. Connect the device.
2. Open Image Capture. You will see that the device name appears on the top left of the screen and your photos appear in the right hand pane.
3. At the bottom left of the screen there is a selection box where you can select the program (if any) you want to open automatically when you connect this device. You can select Image Capture here or any other program that is currently installed on your Mac.

How to import media files from other devices

When you connect a device such as an iPhone, camera or memory stick to your Mac, you can open your photos/media files using Image Capture, which allows you to browse the photos and select those that you want to download. To do this:

1. Open Image Capture (look for Image Capture in Spotlight or open from Finder > Applications)

2. Select the directory where the photos are going to be copied at the bottom of the screen. By default they are imported into "Pictures".

3. If you want to delete the photos from the device once they have been imported, click the "Delete after import" tick box at the bottom left of the screen.

4. If you don't want to import all photos, select the photos to upload, you can select several photos by holding down ctrl while you select the files.

5. Click the "Import" button at the bottom right of the screen if you want to import only the photos selected. If you want to import all photos, select the "Import all" button.

CHAPTER 11 - DISK MANAGEMENT & RECOVERY FUNCTIONS

This section includes some useful information to help you manage your hard drive storage. I am also going to cover a few steps that you will need to follow if you have a major issue with your system and need to recover from backup or re-install your macOS system.

How to check hard drive usage

Go to Apple menu > About this Mac > Storage and the following window will open giving you a summary of the status of your hard drive.

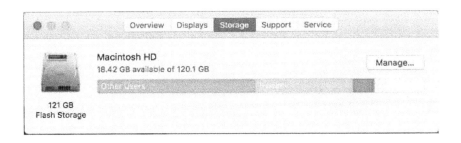

If you have a separate partition for Boot Camp (Windows installation), the space used in this partition will appear in a separate bar so you can see the usage on both partitions.

The window shows you a quick overview of the space available in the drive and the proportion of it currently used by the system (so you cannot delete files from that part).

Storage management features

From macOS Sierra onwards, there are some extra features to help with the management of disk space. You can take a look at the features and configure them by clicking on "Manage" on the screenshot above. The following window pops up:

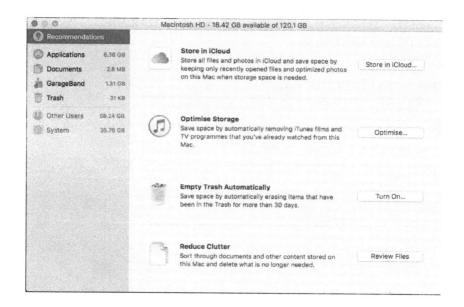

You can enable a number of options to help you manage your hard drive space:

1.   **Store in iCloud**: if you enable this feature, older files and photos will be deleted from your Mac and stored in iCloud, and only more recently used files will remain stored locally on your laptop. You can easily download

any files that you need from iCloud. Potentially this could be a really good way to manage your hard drive space. However, before you enable this feature be aware that Apple only provides 5GB of free space on iCloud, so if you enable this option you will probably need to upgrade your iCloud usage. You can take a look at iCloud's upgrade levels and pricing on Apple's website (http://https://support.apple.com/en-gb/HT201238). I'm not currently using this feature, but as this is still a new feature in macOS I think that if you decide to use it you should check that all the files that you need are stored locally if you intend to travel somewhere where you may not be able to access iCloud.

2. **Optimise storage**: this option will remove any films and TV programs that you have already watched. If you use iTunes to watch films and movies often, it could be a good idea to switch this option on as video files take up a lot of space and remain in your hard drive after you've watched them. You can always download them again if you want to watch them again.

3. **Empty trash automatically**: this feature will automatically delete any files that have been in the trashcan for more than 30 days. I have this feature switched on.

4. **Reduce clutter**: this option presents you with a few options to clear out space on your hard drive. It displays a list of large files so that you can sort through them. You also have access to a file browser where you can

see the various documents and files and their sizes. These browser can be quite useful; it is similar to the Disk Inventory program that I cover below (though Disk Inventory also shows a visual representation of the files). Overall, there are good options to help you clean up your hard drive and manage your disk space.

If you are running out of space or you want to check in more detail how the space is being used or discover the files that are taking up a lot of space on your hard drive you can use option 4 above to "reduce clutter" which provides a breakdown of the space used by each folder and file. However, I like to use a free app, Disk Inventory X (http://www.derlien.com), which provides a breakdown of the space usage in a more graphic way. Bigger files are represented as bigger squares on screen, making it very easy to identify the files that are taking a lot of space.

The program also shows each file type in its own colour: documents in purple, apps in green etc. You can also see the location of a file and its details by clicking on it in the graphic window. So you can easily see the files that are taking up a lot of space on your hard drive, their type and their location.

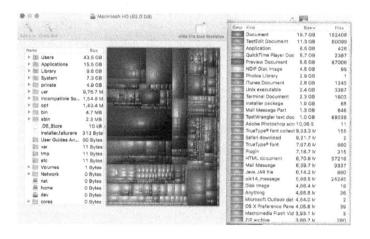

How to recover from system failures

If you are having problems with your Mac (it is not starting properly or it's re-starting continuously for example), you can press Cmd + R as soon as the laptop re-starts (hold for a few seconds until you see the Apple appear on screen). This will launch macOS Utilities with the following options:

1. Restore from Time Machine backup
2. Reinstall macOS
3. Get help online
4. Disk Utility

I have only needed to use this once, it was because I allowed my hard drive to become so full that my Mac was running very slowly, so I had to use Disk Utility to delete a few files.

The options to restore from backup and reinstall can also be very useful if you have a more drastic problem that you are unable to resolve.

CHAPTER 12 - OTHER USEFUL INFO

This section includes some additional information that I have gathered during the last few years while using a Mac: a summary of some of the most useful shortcuts, how to record your screen and the use of dictation among others.

Useful Shortcuts

I don't intend to include an exhaustive list of possible shortcuts that can be used in macOS but to provide some of the shortcuts that I have found most useful. The first thing worth noting is that for many common Windows shortcuts, the Mac shortcut is the same as in Windows but replacing the Ctrl key in Windows with the Cmd key ⌘ in macOS. For example, shortcuts like Ctlr+C in Windows work in macOS as Cmd+C.

Some of the most used keys for shortcuts are:

- Cmd key ⌘
- Shift key ⇧
- Option key, which is the same as Alt ⌥
- Esc key, which is on the top left of the keyboard
- Tab key ⇥

Shortcuts to move a file to a different location:

Cmd + C to copy the file

Cmd + Alt + V to move the file to the new location

Formatting shortcuts

Shortcut	Result
Alt + 3	#
Cmd + C	Copy
Cmd + V	Paste
Cmd + Alt + V	Move (used with Copy)
Cmd + Shift + V	Paste text without formatting
Fn + Delete	Delete text from left to right
Cmd + Ctrl + D	Display definition of the word selected
Cmd+Shift+3	Save a screenshot to file
Cmd+Shift+4	Save a shot of the selected area to file
Cmd+Shift+Ctrl+4	Save a shot of the selected area to the clipboard

Window management shortcuts

Shortcut	Result
Ctrl+Cmd+Spacebar	Show the special characters menu
Cmd+Tab	Show all open apps, toggles between them
Cmd + Alt + Esc	Open force quit application menu
Cmd + Ctrl + Power	Force restart
Cmd + Shift	Toggle between open windows/apps
Cmd+F3	Show Desktop
Cmd + Alt + D	Show/hide the dock
Cmd+minus sign	Zoom out
Cmd+plus sign	Zoom in
Cmd + F	Open a search window
Cmd + Alt + W	Close all windows from active application
Cmd + Alt + H	Hide all applications except the active application
Cmd + i	Opens an information window for a file/folder

Option + Shift + k types the Apple symbol

You'll find many more shortcuts in Apple menu > System Preferences > Keyboard > Shortcuts

You can also find a full list of shortcuts on Apple's support page: http:// support.apple.com/kb/HT1343

How to add your own shortcuts

You can add your own shortcuts following these steps:

1.   Go to Apple menu > System Preferences > keyboard.

2.   Click on shortcuts and select application shortcuts

3.   Click the + symbol and a new menu appears where you can select the

application and the exact menu command you want to include

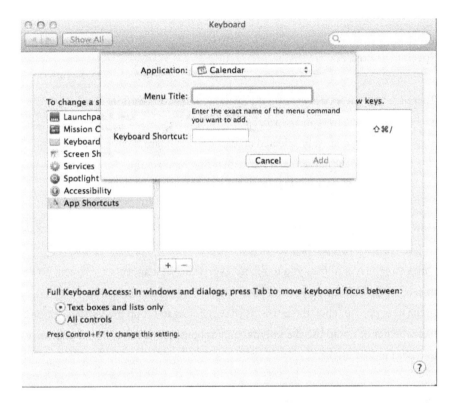

How to activate keyboards

If you use several languages it is really useful to have multiple keyboard input sources, each one enabled for a specific language. An icon on the menu bar allows you to quickly switch between different keyboards. To enable a keyboard input source, follow these steps:

1.   Go to "Apple menu > System Preferences >Keyboard "

2.   Select "input sources" at the top of the screen

3.   Add one or several input sources

4.   Tick the option "Show input menu in the menu bar" at the bottom of the screen

Special characters

There are two ways of accessing the **special characters/emojis** menu:

*   Using the Ctrl+Cmd+Spacebar shortcut.

*   If you have already selected at least one keyboard input source, an icon should appear in the menu bar with a flag representing the current active keyboard. Click on this icon and select "Show emoji & symbols".

How to record your screen

QuickTime player allows you to record everything that appears on screen. To do this, open QuickTime player and go to File>New Screen Recording
In the new pop up, click the arrow as shown below to set up the various options like whether or not to use the internal microphone and whether or not you want to record mouse clicks.

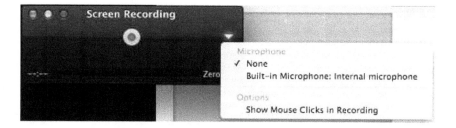

The option to record mouse clicks shows a small circle around the mouse cursor every time you click on something. I found this really useful in videos where you want to show how to perform a certain task on your Mac.

Dictation

Dictation functionality is built into macOS. To enable it, go to the Apple menu > System Preferences > Dictation and speech.

It is possible to enable offline dictation by clicking the option "Use enhanced dictation".

Once you have switched on dictation, you can start using it in most programs by going to the program's menu and to Edit > Start dictation.

Airdrop

Airdrop is a feature in macOS and iOS that allows users to transfer files between Apple devices (MacBook/iPad/iPhone etc.) using Bluetooth or Wi-Fi. I am including a quick guide to Airdrop because I think that when it works it's an easy way to transfer files between devices and/or users. However, I found this feature a bit temperamental, I haven't been able to get it to work consistently. To use it you need to enable either Bluetooth or Wi-Fi and enable Airdrop on both devices. You can enable both of them on your Mac through the menu bar icons. To start Airdrop in your Mac:

1.   Open a Finder window
2.   Select "Airdrop" from the sidebar or Go > Airdrop from the menu bar
3.   You can choose whether to Airdrop only to contacts or to everyone in the option that appears at the bottom of the Airdrop window.
4.   The Airdrop window displays the users that are currently within range.
5.   To share a file with a user drag the file and drop it on the user, then click send.

Picture in picture

In macOS Sierra there is a new "picture in picture" feature that allows you to move a picture from Safari and iTunes to your Desktop, locate it whenever you like within the desktop and re-size it, so that you can easily watch it while you are doing something else, without Safari or iTunes taking extra space on your screen. he bad news is that it doesn't work for YouTube, but it works for every other website I've tried.

Here is an example video window from Safari. You can see the picture on picture icon below. When you click it a separate video only window opens on your Desktop. You can move and re-size the window.

video content
here

00:15 / 00:46

Sign pdf documents

Preview includes a feature that allows you to sign documents using the trackpad. To do this, follow these steps:

1. Right click on the document that you want to sign and select "Open view Preview.app".
2. Go to Tools > Annotate > Signature > Manage signatures.
3. A new window opens up. You have an option to sign your name using the trackpad or sign on a piece of white paper and show the signature to the camera.

Good feature, although I found it quite difficult to create a good signature using the trackpad.

Rename several files at the same time

This feature allows you to rename several files at the same time. To do this, follow the steps below:

1. Open a Finder window.
2. Select the files that you want to rename (you can select several files in Finder pressing the Cmd key at the same time as you select the files).
3. Right click and select "Rename X files" (X indicates the number of files selected).
4. A new dialog box appears with a number of options to rename the files:

- Add text: text can be added before or after the current file name.
- Replace text: selected text in the original name by the new selected text.
- Format: the current file names are replaced by the new format selected. The new formats available are: Name and index, name and counter and name and date. Index, counter and date can be added before or after the name. For example, if I wanted to rename some photos from a trip to London in Dec2016 I could select the "Format" option and choose as name "LondonDec2016" and use an index or a counter starting at 1. The new names would appear as: LondonDec20161.img, LondonDec20162.img and so on.

Useful links

In this section I am going to include some links that I have found useful in the past. If you want to find some more information about a specific feature or need help resolving an issue, there are a number of sites where you can find help:

Useful information

Link	Summary
Apple support communities http:// discussions.apple.com/ welcome	Official community of Apple users where you can search through existing questions and post your own questions.
Apple support page http://support.apple.com	You can access information from Apple about their products: how to use specific features, resolve problems etc. You can also contact their support team if you can't find the answer to your problem.
MacOSX forums http://macosx.com	Community of Apple users where you can search through existing questions and post your own questions.
Macworld http:// www.macworld.co.uk/ how-to/mac/	Website that includes informative articles about different apple products. It includes a how to sections, product reviews, news and deals.
Macrumours http:// www.macrumors.com	Webpage with new about Apple, information about new releases, features etc.

Useful free utilities

Link	Summary
Disk Inventory X http://www.derlien.com	Application to help organise the space in your hard drive. It shows your hard drive usage graphically and allows you to quickly access files and move/delete them. Very useful if you are running out of space.
Avast antivirus https://www.avast.com/ en-gb/mac	Free antivirus and e-mail scanner software.
MSGViewer http://sourceforge.net/ projects/msgviewer/	Software that opens .msg e-mail files.
Onyx http:// www.titanium.free.fr	System maintenance utilities for Mac.
Handbrake http://handbrake.fr	Open source software that coverts video to different formats. If you have a web site this software is really useful to convert videos for web use.
Caffeine http://lightheadsw.com/ caffeine/	Application that stops the Mac from going to sleep or starting the screen saver. Useful for example when you are watching a long video (movie etc).

Other useful free applications

Link	Summary
Evernote http://evernote.com	Software that allows you to take notes, bookmark, download web content, add photos etc. It's available for different platforms so you can install it on your Mac, iPad, iPhone etc and synchronise the data across all different devices. It's a good way to organise all your notes/data. (Evernote is free up to a certain number of transactions per month.)
Gimp http://www.gimp.org	Open Source image editor. It's a free alternative to Photoshop.
Open office http:// www.openoffice.org	Open source office suite similar to MS Office that includes software for word processing, spreadsheets, presentations, graphics and databases.
Textwrangler http:// www.barebones.com/ products/TextWrangler/	Simple text/code editor.

Thank you!

I would like to thank you for purchasing my book and reading it all the way through. I hope you have enjoyed it.

Please take a couple of minutes to provide me with some feedback through a review on Amazon. This will help me understand what you have enjoyed about the book and anything that you think I have missed or could have done better. This will help me to improve, and to continue writing the type of books that you may enjoy reading.

To fill in an **Amazon review** please follow these steps:

1. Go to the Amazon page for the book: http://viewBook.at/switchMac
2. Scroll down to the "Customer Reviews" section.
3. Click on "Write a customer review".
4. Fill in a review for "Switch from PC to Mac".

Is there anything that you would have liked to see in the book that is missing? Do you have any suggestions for any future books or blog posts? **Contact me**: marina@marinagallego.com

Or post your comments through my website: www.maringallego.com

BONUS

I am offering free bonus material accompanying this book which includes over 20 videos showing the step-by-step processes covered in the book. To access the bonus material follow these steps:

1. Go to http://www.marinagallego.com/frompctomac_register
2. Enter your name, username and e-mail.
3. Check the e-mail address provided in step 2. Username and password details to access the bonus data will be e-mailed to your (it may take a couple of minutes).
4. Once you have your login details, click on the link in the e-mail or go back to http://www.marinagallego.com and click on the Login link on the top right of your screen. Enter your login details.
5. Go to the navigation bar on the top of the web page and select "Videos". This will take you to the page with the video content.

If after 5-10min you have not received the registration e-mail, please check your spam folder. If you have any problems, please either use the contact page on my website or e-mail admin@marinagallego.com and we will come back to you as soon as possible.

Acknowledgements

I would like to thank all my friends and family for their support to write this book. Special thanks to my dear friend Giulia who has supported me throughout this project. I would not have been able to finish this book without her.

Thank you all!

Glossary

Airdrop is a feature in macOS and iOS that allows users to transfer files between multiple Apple devices (MacBook/iPad/iPhone).

Airplay allows you to mirror your Mac or iOS device's screen on your TV or other screen if you have an Apple TV device.

Dock is a bar at the bottom of the screen in macOS that shows your favourite applications as well as any other open applications and the Trashcan.

ExFAT is a file system that can be read and written in both Windows and macOS.

FaceTime is an apple application that allows voice and video calls between Apple devices.

FAT32 is a file system that can be read and written in both Windows and macOS. It has a number of limitations; files cannot be bigger than 4GB and the overall partition cannot be bigger than 32GB.

FileVault is an encryption program included in macOS.

Finder is the file manager in macOS.

Gatekeeper is a security feature within macOS that allows you to control the origin of the applications that are downloaded to your Mac. Enabling this option helps protect your Mac against malware.

HFS (Hierarchical File System) is a file system developed by Apple, it is the default file system for macOS.

iTunes is a media manager application developed by Apple that allows you to store and play both audio and video files.

iBooks is Apple's electronic book application.

Keychain is a password management system included with macOS.

Launchpad enables quick access to applications in your Mac.

Menu bar is the bar on the top of your Mac's Desktop that allows access to the Apple menu, the current application's menu and a number of additional features like Wi-Fi/Bluetooth/Battery status, keyboard options and Time Machine.

Migration Assistant is an application built into macOS that allows the user to transfer key files (documents folder, bookmarks etc) between two Mac machines or between a PC and a Mac.

Mission Control allows the user to see and organise all the open windows into one or several Desktops.

NTFS is a Windows proprietary file system. macOS can read NTFS but not write to it.

Safari is the default browser in macOS.

Siri is a voice-activated program on Apple devices that allows you to perform a number of operations like finding files, writing e-mails or finding information on the web.

Smart Folder is a special type of folder where the contents are defined by a specified search criteria.

Spotlight is a search utility in macOS that can be accessed through the menu bar.

Tags are a feature in macOS that allows you to categorise files.

Time Machine is a backup utility built in to macOS.

Trackpad is the mouse-type functionality built into Apple computers.